HOW TO BE
SOMEBODY

The

Nordic Inn

© LOONART DESIGNS   L 37

YETTA BERNHARD

HOW TO BE
SOMEBODY

BFI Publications
Brookline, Massachusetts

First printing: by Celestial Arts April 1975   ISBN 0-89087-020-9
Second printing: by Celestial Arts June 1975
Third printing: by BFI Publications October 1984
Manufactured in the United States of America

Library of Congress Cataloging in Publications Data

Bernhard, Yetta, 1909–
     How to be Somebody

        1. Maturation (Psychology). 2. Self-acceptance
1. Title
BF710.B47   158.1   74-24994
ISBN 0-930017-01-3

1   2   3   4   5

To Joseph Harry Bernhard
Who helped me to be somebody

Foreword

Despite the title, this is not a "how to" book in the strictest sense of the words. The editors have selected universal questions based on the fact that many of us, at some time or another in our lives, have felt unloved, isolated, friendless, lonely, or depressed. My friend and respected colleague, Yetta Bernhard, addresses herself to these questions in the down-to-earth, common sense manner that is typical of her perceptive and intuitive style as a therapist.

So it is that you, the reader, will get a sense of what it is like to be with a gifted therapist. If you have ever felt any of the kinds of feelings reflected by the questions in the pages that follow, this book can do much more than entertain or edify you. It is quite possible that if you can hear what she is saying, you will be able to change your opinion of yourself. It is also possible that you can change your ability to be with other people. It is even possible that understanding what Yetta Bernhard is talking about when she talks of self care will give you the ability, courage, and direction to change the course of your life.

—*Virginia Satir*

Preface

First, I would like to explain the person-specific work involved in being somebody. It doesn't just happen. You make it happen.

To be somebody means:

Focusing on a goal—both short-term and long-term,

Assessing possible areas of work along the path to the goal,

Making a decision of commitment to work on that same path,

Carrying out the decisions necessary to reach the goal through specific behavior,

Assessing its practicality by experiencing its workability,

Learning from mistakes along the path to the goal,

Making new decisions and choosing new alternatives as they are needed,

Developing frustration tolerance for rejection (which can only be accomplished by risk-taking),

Accepting the reality of pain and separation as a "given" in living.

In addition, to me, a "somebody" connotes a feeling of self-worth and importance as a person in spite of imperfections.

As for myself, I know my strengths and I enjoy them. I know that I have weaknesses and I try to make them as little destructive as possible.

I know that I can't sing because I can't carry a tune. I don't deprecate myself because I can never be an opera singer.

I know I have unusual powers of concentration, and I enjoy that. It is very productive.

I know I am not an athlete, and I don't blame myself for not keeping up in the pool or on the track, or whatever. I love to listen to good music, and I appreciate my sense of appreciation for good music. But it is an agony for me to play the piano. But I don't blame myself for not being able to perform musically.

I know I like many people, and I know I don't care for others. I am also aware that not everyone likes me. I cannot give and I cannot get total approval, and I come to terms with that. I know I am a human being and as such, I know I will "goof"—hopefully not too frequently. I know that "goofs" can be learning processes.

I hope I make them so.

—*Yetta M. Bernhard*

HOW TO BE
SOMEBODY

How to be somebody starts with a decision and an assessment of self: *"I count."* This means that I am important enough to invest the work and pain it takes to:

1. change the behavior patterns that sabotage me,
2. take the necessary risks of self-assertion,
3. develop interest beyond immediate personal concerns,
4. bring *meaning* into my life.

It was upon such work as this that the art of self-care developed.

To be a somebody not only means validating myself as a person, but also means making impact on others in specific relationships. Interactions often produce conflict. Conflict need not be lethal. It can be managed productively for mutual benefit and growth.

The tools and ammunition developed for the productive management of conflict evolved in my therapeutic application as a system of responsible self-care—an individual growth process and a relationship growth process. I maintain that the practice of self-care is the process by and through which self-respect, self-worth, and self-liking are developed.

This involves an investment of work in:
deepening of awareness of self,
assessing cost of goals set,
and risking hurt and rejection.

Such an investment in work gives an impactful message:

I am worth bothering about!

In order to practice self-care, one must be aware of one's own tension, stresses, conflicts, pains, and deprivations, and be able to take the responsibility of dealing with them. This includes looking for alternatives and other choices of action different from those currently unsatisfactory ones. It means risking the impact of authenticity. It is a process by which we enhance a relationship. The focus is my responsibility to myself and to my relationship with significant others.

Self-care means:
detective work on one's self,
daring to be,
risking another's displeasure,
maintaining areas of privacy,
accepting limitations,
realistically assessing "shoulds" and
"oughts,"
and creating areas of power.

It means actively taking full responsibility for yourself in meeting needs, attaining goals, and in making relationships.

I don't really know who I am. At work I seem to be somebody whom more positive personalities can manipulate to get things done. At home I am thought of as the provider and little more. I feel trapped between my job and my responsibilities. I rarely seem to have wants that I can fulfill for myself. How can I really be me?

You are talking about wants. Therefore, you have something specific in mind. What wants are you talking about? Wants for companionship, affection, closeness, leisure time? Wants for what? What it sounds like is that you are expecting something or somebody else to do for you what is your responsibility to do for yourself.

*But how do I do that? How do I
strike out for myself when I am so
used to having other people push
me around?*

Other people can push you around only by your
consent and your collusion. If you are saying "I'm
pushed" into conforming to another's wants, focus on
specific incidents that illustrate this. Then commit
yourself to more authentic responses—saying "no" to
requests you don't want to go along with. As I see it, the
power to say no and mean it or to offer a more
compatible choice, frees you to be; to take care of yourself. So, when and where and how are you pushed
around? What are the specifics? What are your
alternatives? And what risks do you take in this self-
assertive behavior?

*I always seem to do what everybody
else wants me to do. I want to be
liked, so I am afraid to say no,
because if I do I'm afraid people
won't like me.*

This is very possible— that people won't like you
when you say no. Temporarily they won't like you
because you're frustrating them. And anyone who is
frustrated does not enjoy it, but that is part of the
relationship. And if you want to have a relationship, then
you have to learn how to tolerate the frustration in
yourself, and the frustrating of others at necessary times.

You have already indicated that attempting to
please *everybody* at all times results in not pleasing yourself. You seem to have experienced the cost in self-denial
of that behavior pattern. I suspect you have a feeling of
enslavement and are seeking to throw off these self-
imposed shackles.

What I really want is self-respect.
How can I get it?

You see, you actually erase yourself when you program yourself just to please the other, whether or not it be for fear of being disliked, or fear of "rocking the boat," whatever. You are not being authentic. You are really conning the other person into thinking that what you are saying and doing is actually what you want to be saying and doing. That kind of self-erasure brings absolutely no dividends, because to you in your guts, a sacrifice for the other means expectation of a reward. And when the other person doesn't know you are sacrificing, there can't be a reward. So no reward is forthcoming and you are angry as the dickens and you pile up a bag of resentment against the other person.

The other side of this coin is to accommodate to expand yourself. This may open you to interests that you didn't think you had at all.

You open this kind of experience for yourself. You say so out front because the person with whom you are engaging is more important to you than "doing your own thing." You simply say "I don't like to go to the ball game," or "I don't like the ballet," or "I don't like this television program, but I really like sitting by your side. Maybe I'll sleep through it, but I want to be by your side." That is an out-in-front self-acknowledgment, not a self-erasure. That is when accommodation "smells like a rose."

The only way I know of attaining self-respect is

through self-honoring. This entails the risk of being disliked at times. You have to risk saying no, no matter how afraid you are to say it. What dire things will happen to you if you hurt these other people? Will they be able to stand it? People are not as fragile as we sometimes think.

A possible first assignment for you to consider would be for an entire week risk being authentic. Refrain from accommodation just "to be liked." Consider the experience of saying, "I'm not available," or "I am not able to do this at this time." After a week of practice, if the feeling is one of great self-appreciation, renegotiate this commitment to yourself week by week until it becomes a new pattern of behavior.

In the practice of saying your necessary "nos" and setting your necessary limitations, you are engaging in the work of breaking an old, well-learned and well-established behavior pattern. This is the process by which you create the power to do what you don't feel like doing, but *want to do;* a process of working over feelings, of extending yourself beyond the content of your guts into more productive behavior.

Consider commiting yourself to a new tactic of living for one week. At the end of the week renegotiate with yourself—to continue on this road or to modify the commitment according to your experiential learning. In addition, explore your inner world and ask yourself what impact other than "provider" do you want to make on your family. Start communicating this information and see whether or not there is enough good will and interest to work at this as a family project.

If I can do this for a week, and I get
this self-respect—will I be able to
like myself more?

That is an inevitable evolutionary process as you
validate yourself as a human being. And that means not
only setting limitations, but accepting yourself as a
human being with the right to "goof."

I hate to goof.

Of course. But as soon as you stop competing with
God—which is the only symbol of perfection that I
know—and perfection is an ideal; something to strive
toward, a constant process of growth, not attainment of
perfection, then you can come to terms with your own
humanness and expect yourself to goof. Not to
deliberately goof, of course, but not expect yourself to be
perfect. Then with the expectation not to be perfect, you
open the possibility of learning from your imperfections.
Every time you make an error, you don't waste that error
provided you learned from it what *not* to do next
time—or how to do better next time. And implicit in all
of this is also the concept of self-forgiveness for not being
perfect.

*If I achieve self-respect, will I be
able to know myself then?*

The only way I know to know yourself is to set
yourself tasks that you think are reasonable and in the
carrying out, validate their reasonableness or unreason-
ableness—their "fit" or "misfit." "Did I bite off more
than I can chew? If so, I have to re-evaluate and
re-program myself according to my physical, mental,
and emotional abilities."

Again, we are into this business of making decisions
and finding out how appropriate and effective the
decisions are through living them—putting them into
action.

That will be very hard to do.

Yes. And if living were an easy job and wanted relationships came automatically, then I would have no profession. At least not this profession. We do have to be educated to communicate effectively with one another, and to communicate effectively with one another means the risking of a certain amount of openness. Really say what you feel. And by this I don't mean, "You are a son of a bitch for pushing me," but instead, "*I* feel pushed. *I* feel harrassed when such-and-such happens. Therefore, I can only do so much at this time." You see, a sense of identity comes, I believe, when you take the risk of making decisions that you need to make and carry them out. No matter how many "nos" are involved.

*I see. What we are really talking
about here is self-care, isn't it?*

Yes. And this is one way in which it works. If I say to
myself, for example, that I have to study for this
examination next week, or I have to do this or that job—
whatever it is, I make a program. I make a work
program for myself, and somehow or other, a crisis takes
place and I can't carry it out. Then I assess the situation
at the deadline and consider the alternatives or choices
that I have. When one door is closed, how many other
doors can I open in order to do effectively what I need to
do? This goes for a job, and it goes for human relations,
too. I could commit myself to a family problem, a social
problem, or whatever, and then find in the course of
living out the experience that there were some missing
factors I wasn't aware of before that affect what I'm
trying to do. So I become aware of what choices or
alternatives I have, and I use every crisis or disappointment as a specific problem to which I must find a
solution and with which I must deal.

*It seems to me that if I take myself
into consideration as much as
self-care implies, then I run the risk
of being considered selfish.*

As I see it, implicit in the meaning of the word,
"selfish" is *exploitation* of another human being. Self-
care never exploits another human being—it is never at
the expense of another human being. Self-care is a self-
honoring, not a self-indulging. Although self-care may
have aspects of self-indulgence at the same time they are
very healthy and productive aspects of self-indulgence.

Self-care puts the responsibility where it needs to be.
I am the captain of my ship. And if I am a "victim of
circumstances" that can only be by my permission. If I
am manipulated or emasculated that can only be by my
permission. I let it happen. Self-care means you have the
responsibility *not* to let these things happen. *You* have
the responsibility. And that includes including yourself
where you want to be included, and excluding yourself
when necessary.

You are at a gathering, for example, and you feel
left out. It is your responsibility to include yourself and
not wait for an invitation like a helpless, dependent
infant. This is all part of what I mean by, "You are
responsible for attaining what you think is important and
productive." If you stand at the wayside and wait for
something to happen, you are just going to be standing at
the wayside forever.

You see, self-care involves the risk-taking of being

accepted or rejected. There is no way of living that I know without the accompaniment of the pain of being rejected as well as the happiness of being accepted at times.

If you want a changed behavior, you have to make it happen. To make it happen, you have to commit yourself to work, because your mind tells you, "This is the goal I want." And after you engage in a productive behavior often enough, the guts and the head become more congruent.

And then you have the possibility of spontaneity when it's thoroughly learned; when the behavior becomes thoroughly familiar. When it is thoroughly familiar, it's easy. When it is easy, it can be spontaneous. You can't be spontaneous with something new. To learn to walk is a difficult procedure. The baby stands up and makes a hesitant step and sits down again. And you have to encourage him. Soon he stands and then he runs. Only because he has learned to use his legs well can he spontaneously run. Hopefully, we are all in new learning processes.

I want to like myself, but I can't.
My life is spent riding to a job I
don't particularly care for. My day
is spent with strangers who never
speak, and then I return to a wife
who doesn't care for her job, either.
She is nothing more than my house-
keeper. We are mostly silent
together, having little to
communicate. And in this state we
have few friends. How can I be
expected to like myself under these
conditions?

What you have just said is that you both are
contributing to the lack of communication because you
said you were both silent together. In order to break such
an impasse, it is your responsibility to communicate.
You sound frustrated. Say so. You sound empty. Say so.
And then challenge yourself. "What would make my life
less empty?"

You have the very practical consideration of the
necessity of working at a job which does not particularly
interest you in order to get the wherewithal to live—to
exist. All right. So what compensating factors—what
"goodies" can you give yourself? In this case, you need to
attain the wherewithal to buy your food, clothing, and to
keep a roof over your head. If there is an opportunity,
consider changing jobs or invest in the idea of changing
jobs. It would take time, money, and energy to change

jobs. But if these things are practical, explore them. There are hundreds of different ways you can make your life more interesting outside of the comparatively limited time you spend at work. Eight hours a day are spent working, and eight hours are spent sleeping. That's sixteen. You still have eight hours of possible fun and more kinds of nourishment—intellectual, emotional, and physical.

Under the conditions you mention, the basis for self-liking is absent because there seems to be no responsibility taken for self-care. You sound as if you are a helpless victim of circumstances.

I suspect you are not that helpless. It seems you have already taken the first step out of your morass. I am talking about recognizing that a problem exists. You have recognized it and now challenge yourself to do something about it. I foresee specific questions you may consider answering in relation to specific areas of your living.

Job

1. Is this job I am not particularly interested in a *dead end* for me?
2. What are the possibilities of changing this job?
3. What avenues do I explore?
4. What is the cost of change in time, energy, and money?
5. How can I make this present job more interesting?

Lack of Communication with Wife

Dare I take the initiative in opening communication by risking disclosures such as, "I feel empty." "My life has no meaning." "There is no joy in our relationship."

These are the inner messages I suspect that might be the opening door of mutual contact.

1. What specific responsibility do I take to change the atmosphere of our intimate living?
2. What new interest can I or we explore?
3. How do we go about making friends?
4. What organizations, societies, or groups (church, school, civic, political, or social organizations) offer opportunities to expand our horizons and make contact with people?

Take responsibility for your own self-care. Acknowledging the problem is the first step. Doing something about it is the next step.

*What has happened is that we have
got ourselves into a rut. We seem to
be imprisoned in our own boxes.
And every time I try to say anything
to her, or she to me about how
empty and alone we feel, we get
into a fight.*

This sounds like a "Poor Us" game. Oh, how empty
and isolated and alone we feel! It sounds as if you are
putting blame and responsibility on each other's
shoulders—passing the buck.

I say, what are the ways and means of *not* being
empty, isolated, or alone? That means investing in the
pain of change; including the effort itself, which can be
pain. Any new kind of experience, by its very newness, is
strange. Strangeness does seem somewhat fearful and
scary. But it becomes less fearful and scary as you
become more and more accustomed to doing for yourself.
For example, "we are so friendless." What are possible
interests that will open avenues of friendship? If you are
religiously inclined, there are certainly churches and
synagogues. If you are athletically inclined, there are all
kinds of athletic organizations. There are all kinds of
civic, political and social organizations where people of
similar interests gather. Research and investigate,
tasting new experiences. This doesn't come without
effort, and you have to ask yourself if you are worth the
effort.

*What if I feel that I am not worth
the effort? I think that that is where
the problem has been.*

Then, enjoy your inactivity! Enjoy your isolation!
The pay-off of the conclusion, "I am not worth the
effort," absolves you from any responsibility to work at
change.

I guess I deserved that. But what about our fights?

Obviously your fights have led nowhere. They do not seem to have given any new information or led to any new alternatives. Your fights seem to be mutual "blame sessions."

Let's take a specific issue you both agree is a mutual bone of contention. You say, "we seem to be imprisoned in our own boxes." You built your own prisons, now how do you get out of them? If you approach this as a problem to be solved, you avoid the setting of blame or fault. You avoid defensive, acid encounters.

What doors can you open?

      Civic

      Political

      Recreational

      Educational

      Social

By mutual agreement, in what avenues of exploration do you commit yourself to engage? You cannot change a long-term pattern of unproductive behavior and attitude overnight. There is no magic formula to guarantee miracles. When you turn a "fight" into a problem-solving challenge, focusing on a specific issue of conflict, you may be changing the atmosphere of intimate living from that of two adversaries (one against the other) to that of two partners (one for and with the other).

As soon as you change a relationship from that of

adversaries in a power and assessing "fault" struggle to one of authentic confrontation and negotiation as a mutual growth process, you are out of the win-lose arena and into that of mutual expansion through authentic being. This is a process involving self-care, awareness of the other, and enactment of whatever disciplines that are necessary to meet common goals.

And I never said it would be easy.

*People don't like me. I can see it in
their faces, hear it in the slighting
remarks that they make. So, I tell
myself, "What the hell! Who
cares?" I dress and act as though I
don't give a damn and admit that
I'm thoroughly disorganized in
everything I try. But I know deep
inside that I do give a damn. I'd
like very much to be friendly and
warm with people. Can a
psychology of this kind be
changed?*

Only through your behavior.

Let's pick up on what we can immediately do about
this. You say, "I am disorganized," and you say, "I dress
deliberately to turn people off," because I violate their
standards of dress acceptability, etc. Disorganization is
not an incurable disease, and when you are individual-
istic enough to violate another person's standards, it is a
little foolhardy to expect acceptance when you dishonor
the other's value system. A certain amount of respect for
my value system is implicit in the relationship, if we are
going to have a relationship. So, what are you saying? On
whose terms am I accepted? First, turn to yourself. How
important is it to you and what is the meaning of your

disorganization? Does it hurt enough to suffer the work entailed in becoming more organized? How important is it for you to dress as if you don't give a damn? So, if you *do* give a damn, dress accordingly!

You see, what you are doing is deliberately creating an image that is self-sabotaging, because it violates your own value system. So you are actually programming yourself for the disaster that you have. Any program can be re-programmed, you know.

*This is what is so hard. It seems as
if you have to find some middle
area between being a doormat and
a closed door, and that's very hard
to find.*

Exactly. Let's start with the things that you are dissatisfied with about yourself. Never mind somebody else's response to you. Let's start with *you.* You are disorganized; you dress as if you don't give a damn. These are two things that you have said. All right, how are you disorganized? Give me the specifics. And then give yourself a test. What is the most important thing in this disorganization that hurts you and sabotages you the most?

*It just seems as though I never have
time to do the things that I want to
do. It seems as if time is slipping by
and I have no control over what
happens in that time.*

All right. Give me a schedule of a whole day. What
do you do with the time? List your tasks in hierarchical
order—in order of their importance. What absolutely
must be done today? Limit this to one given day, and
when you get one day in control the rest of them will tend
to follow. You will have started a new pattern. You will
have to make the effort; it won't happen automatically.
And it won't happen overnight. You will be working on a
time budget that may need adjustments from day to
day—in the process of which you practice new disciplines
and include in the time budget specific minimal space for
doing a thing you want to do.

*I see. What you are telling me is
that this psychology is not going to
be changed. I am.*

Exactly. You and your behavior are related. The set
tasks that you commit yourself to do, you then do, and
you find out realistically what is possible and workable.

*Everything you have said to me
seems to involve trust—trust of
myself, and trust of other people
and their value systems. How can I
build trust, especially after I have
acted as if I don't give a damn for
so long?*

The only way I know to build trust is *to act as if you
are trusting.* This means taking the risk of
disappointment, betrayal, disillusionment, and pain. It
may be the means of making a relationship meaningful
and lasting, or it may be the means of breaking the
relationship. There is a potential possibility of intimacy
or alienation. When one's self-care is in conflict with
another's value system, separation may be the road to
self-validation, responsibility, and growth.

To trust means to be willing to gamble that the other
is trustworthy. But to my way of thinking, "as if trust" is
well worth the risk. In reality, I see nothing to lose,
because you either make possible something worthwhile
between you, or find that nothing worthwhile was
possible. Trusting does not guarantee trustworthiness.

The kinds of negotiations involved in "as-if" trust
depend on the specific areas of distrustfulness involved.
Before we can successfully act as if we trust another, we
often need to work on our trust in ourselves. Many of my
initial exercises in as-if trust are exercises in self-care.

People need to learn to take responsibility for their own personal well-being before they can begin to practice trusting their partners. Building a solid emotional base of your own worth by taking responsibility for self-care eliminates the possibility of falling apart in case trust of another is misplaced. Your own structure stands secure in spite of hurt.

Incidentally, never forget that the phrases "May I?" or "Will you permit it?" are bridges to another person. Also, conflicting ways of doing and thinking are not to be judged as "right" or "wrong" but as differences to be tolerated, changed, or negotiated. They form an acknowledgment of mutual rights, permission to be different, to see things differently, and to keep the relationship. And in the enacting of this, you will show, truly, that you do give a damn.

*I am a very angry and frustrated
young woman. I want to be
somebody as a woman, but have
felt throughout all my life that I
have been subjugated. I can't do
the kinds of things I want to do and
I don't make enough money
because I am a woman. How do I
get out of that trap? How do I stand
up for myself and make myself
heard without sounding strident or
whining?*

Can you be more specific?

Yes. What I am really thinking
about is my relationship with my
husband. He treats me as if I'm a
not-too-bright pet. His attitude is,
well, you're only a woman, so I
don't expect anything better. Then
I find myself conforming to that
role he has assigned me and hating
myself for it and not knowing how
to get out.

He can only assign you a role if you accept that role.
He can assign and you can rebel. If yours is a subservient
role, what is the nature of the subservience?

When it comes to a big decision
about what we are going to do,
where we are going on vacation,
how we are going to raise our
children, it's just as if I don't have a
voice. Sometimes I am seen as a
lover, sometimes as a mother,
sometimes as a wife. But I am not
seen as a person. And when I stand
up and say that I want to be seen as
a person, we get into a fight.

What do you want—specifically?

*I want to go back to college. But my
husband sees this only in terms of
my neglecting my duties.*

All of what you do depends upon how much courage
you have to validate yourself. This is the art of living that
I am talking about all the time. If you really want to go
back to college, and the obstacle is the statement that
you are neglecting your duties, ask some questions.
What duties are you neglecting? Who is being neglected?
If it is your duty to have dinner at a certain time, and the
people for whom you are preparing dinner can well serve
themselves, then it is just a question of organization and
management with which you have to deal. The whole
business of setting limitations is part of the art of living,
and something with which we must all come to terms if
we are to live together in any semblance of harmony.

So you may have to face the statement that you are
neglecting your duties with the retort, "I am absolving
myself from these duties!" And then you make a new list
of duties that may inconvenience your family, but it
certainly won't sabotage them.

After years of being served in a particular manner
and the service is suddenly withheld, of course you are
going to get criticism and resentment and conflict. Now
you must ask yourself, is my goal important enough to
withstand the criticism and resentment and conflict?

And how can I re-educate my family in order to validate the direction in which I want to go. If the cost of this direction is minimal discomfort on the part of your family, it may well be worth that cost. You make the stand. And if you intend to make a stand without creating waves, that is a fantasy. The waves are the price you may have to pay. Is it worth it?

*I've tried to be somebody in so
many ways. When I was a child I
wanted very much to win the love of
my parents. I did everything I could
to please them, but it always
seemed to me that they liked my
older brother much better. How
can I get over this lifelong feeling
that I'm in second place?*

First of all, this is your perception, and it is the
perception of a young, dependent child and the world
about him—his parents. A client told me a similar
grievance. And interestingly enough, we were fortunate
enough to have his older brother present. The parents
died. The brother's comment when he heard this story of
being in second place was, "What a lot of hogwash! *I* was
the fall guy in the family! All of the responsibility fell
onto *my* shoulders! I was the one asked to do it, to carry
the responsibility to do the job—to take care of you. Our
father wasn't favoring me—he was *using* me to safeguard
you, so that life would be easier for you. Because I was
older *I* had to take more of the responsibility because you
were so young. What you saw as being favoring, I saw as
being exploiting of me!"

So, the first job we had was to check out all of the
perceptions involved for reality fit. Is my perception of
the world your perception of the world? Are we seeing the
same thing? In other words, how I see things must be
checked out against how you see the same thing.
Our perceptions are subjective reactions and very person-
specific, depending upon one's own value system and ego
strength.

An important conflict area can arise from the failure to communicate expectations people have of one another. "Proper" ways of behavior in a relationship are *assumed* to be so well known that the possibility of different concepts is not considered. My "shoulds" are assumed to be your "shoulds." In effect, this kind of an assumption acts as a script which one expects the other to know automatically without handing over the details—exposing the script.

Again, this has to do with reality fit. A reading of expectations one has of the other is an exercise in checking out reality fit, as well as giving information about the expectations. Out of this mutual reading exchange, issues of conflict may arise. What is expected may not be possible for the other to give. Limitations of each have to be clearly defined and other alternatives and choices considered.

So in this case, we would really research the situation and check it out. We soon would determine whether there was a reality fit or not. but whether there was or was not a reality fit, the job remains the same. You have imprinted yourself with the concept that you are in second place. All too often this is what we do to ourselves—not what somebody else does to us. Then, if we have imprinted ourselves with the concept that we are always in second place how do we put ourselves into first place?

We have to ask ourselves the very important question. What makes me feel in first place? In intimate living, for example, what do I want from my mate? What would make me feel in first place? As soon as I find out what I want, then it becomes my responsibility to say so, and we're right in the midst of a job of self-care.

This means saying, for instance, "When I come home to a smile and a warm greeting I feel important— really significant in your life." This is an "I" message that informs. Another message might be, "Before you make a social engagement with family, friends or business associates, check it out with me. That makes me feel I count."

Another means of putting yourself in first place is to be aware of your irritations, frustrations, humiliations and angers and to take the courage to verbalize these feelings in a manner that gives information without a "put-down" to another person. Such comments as : "I felt irritated at having to wait for you when I was ready to keep an important date;

"I was frustrated when there was no follow-up on what you promised to do;

"I was humiliated when you "jokingly" made fun of me;

"I was angry when you interfered at the time I was dealing with the kids my way—which was certainly not harmful to the kids."

These statements are all "I" messages and may open the way to reducing the acid content of the feelings expressed.

When you say what you feel, you are exposing what *is,* and it is the first step to doing something about what you feel. When you carry it to the next step, and do something about it, you are saying, "I am worth bothering about. I am important enough to bother about." And when you bother about yourself, you are making yourself important. You are making of yourself a *somebody.*

The problem is I feel like a nobody.
How can I feel like somebody? How
can I attain happiness?

This can be a slow and painful process of self-exploration. We may start at it negatively. What makes you unhappy—feel like a "nobody?" We don't know what makes you happy yet. But we know that you are unhappy. What makes you unhappy and what can we do about it? Where we begin the self-exploration depends upon where you are.

Generally speaking, "to be happy" is a Utopian expectation. To work at making differences less painful is to set realistic goals with specific ways and means of attaining such goals, to critically assess one's self and a relationship may be the means of attaining more happiness and minimizing pain.

To be more specific, happiness is a result of self-validation, as I see it: self-honoring. Happiness is the result of being at peace with yourself. Happiness is a result of a pride in accomplishment that is recognized. Happiness is a result of a productive relationship, of productive being. Happiness is the result of the created ability to expand yourself beyond the limitations of your own person, and own immediate concerns, into the concerns of the world and another person. How can you validate yourself? Research ways and means. What relationship do you want to improve? What are your resources? How do you use them? What input are you willing to invest? What in this world concerns you? What responsibilities do you take?

When I went to school I was
haunted by the idea that I wasn't
worthy. My teachers made me feel
that I couldn't learn. What I
desperately needed was positive
support and encouragement of the
idea that I could learn, because I
knew that I could—and have since
proved it. Now that I understand
more of myself, what can I do to
overcome the feelings of inferiority
that have been bred into me?

You have already made a step. When you make the positive statement that you have proved it, that you know you could learn, that is a giant step forward.

*Why is it so easy to feel bad about
ourselves? Why do we all tend to do
that?*

Because it may be that somewhere in our Judeo-
Christian ethic we all picked up the belief that the ideal
was really attainable: total selflessness and total
perfection. As human beings, total selflessness in
practical effect means total slavery. It means slavery to
someone else, to some other thing; the ideal, a person,
whatever. Total selflessness is total slavery and the
history of all slavery is the history of rebellion. The idea of
total selflessness is destructive because it is not human
and only God is perfect. I don't attempt to compete with
God! A human being is an *imperfect* being, and the
growth process is to learn from our imperfections and
goofs. In other words, our imperfections and goofs may
very well be, if we make them so, productive in the
learning they entail. All living is productive when it is a
growth process.

I would not concentrate on the "why" of the feeling.
You cannot program feeling. You *can* program behavior.
You can act *As If* you are important. And such behavior,
when consistent and persistent, may well—in
time—change the feeling of inferiority to one of worth.

I think of two examples of this kind of thing from
my practice. I once knew an architect who went out of his
way—over two miles—in order to avoid seeing a
particular building that violated his sense of proportion,
his sense of balance, his whole artistic concept of what

ought to be. This was sensitivity to a rather unusual degree.

In order to build more freedom of movement on his part (this was only one instance of many other self-imposed and self-developed limitations) we used a particular method as a practice session in change. For a period of months he accepted the assignment to not only pass this particular building every day, but to safely park for a minute or so in front of it. The object of this was to build a frustration tolerance toward what he had convinced himself that he couldn't tolerate. In a comparatively brief period of time—about two or three months— he attained a tolerance for this building in such a way that it didn't even raise his temperature.

The new tolerance was a release from a self-imposed constriction—a new created freedom.

I think the most classic example I can give, and the most unusual one is the one that follows. A couple came to me. The woman was estranged from her husband physically. She could no longer tolerate his physical touch, and yet she wanted to maintain the relationship. It gave her status and it gave her economic security and these were her two prime values. One could stand aside and judge right here, and say what crass motives for maintaining a relationship! I say, do away with these judgments and just attend to a goal that is not harmful to either party. This is what happened in this case. The husband was becoming more and more alienated and was beginning to look into other pastures. But there was enough interest and love on his part to want to work at the relationship. She had closed the door to other sexual relationships, no matter how tempting, because she didn't want to lose her place in the world, in her society, which her husband provided.

So they were faced with reaching the goal of intimate relationship which the woman said she wanted, in spite of her physical aversion to the very act in which she wanted to engage. So we started the process of behavior modification—actually conditioning her to accept that which she was feeling averse to accepting. Little by little, at first just tolerating a touch, in just a little over a year, she was again becoming familiar with closeness in a series of slow, consistent physical contact, from the least threatening to more and more physical closeness, through familiarity. Not only was sexual union attained, but in spite of the seemingly questionable reason for attainment, and based on a long period of care and consideration of another person, there was a new quality in the relationship. They attained new dividends—feelings of warmth, affection, and love. This is the most dramatic case of acting over feeling to attain a feeling that is wanted in my experience.

*I see. But those two people had
professional help. Can you do it by
yourself?*

    I did not do the work. They did. I acted as a catalyst
to provoke change. I helped them find for themselves
what was possible to do.

*I think it's extremely hard to
validate yourself in this culture. We
are so often met with rejection.*

    What rejection?

*The artist who does a beautiful
painting and can't sell it. The
writer who writes a fine novel and
every publisher turns it down. The
woman who had high hopes for her
children and they turn into school
dropouts and jailbirds. These are
the kinds of rejections I mean.*

I look at these as not necessarily rejections, but as disappointments in living. When acknowledgment of our skills is dependent on marketing judgments and acceptances of others, we do have realistic trouble. This is a very legitimate grief and a very legitimate reality.

You see, again, we are into the whole problem of what other doors can we open when specific doors are closed. And if we have only one road to accomplishment, happiness or heaven, we are in trouble, or sick. But we can all research our own resources and find other outlets for our energies and abilities. It is a question of exploration and opening new doors over and over again. There are always choices and always alternatives. The work of living is to find them.

*Few people I've met seem to under-
stand their own tensions and
conflicts. They only appear to know
when they are feeling good or bad.
There is nothing in between—and
apparently no growth. I'm one of
this grey mass of people. I spend
most of my time seeking pleasure
and avoiding pain. Without my
cigarettes, alcohol, and television
set I'd be lost. Can that be all there
is to life?*

Yes, that may be all there is to life, if the main
thrust of it is to avoid pain. Because that means you are
only half-living. Living involves pain and joy. Living in a
relationship is what we are talking about, and since
productive living has no room for mutual slavery, we are
going to frustrate each other by stopping negative impact
or encroachment upon one another. And the frustration
and the limitations may be very painful at times. We are
not always available to one another when we need one
another, and that is painful. But it is not destructive
unless we make it so. We have far more resources than
we allow ourselves to utilize.

Everything seems to lead us back to the concept of self-care. Would you think it would be fair to say that unless you live out self-care, self-honoring, that you cannot have a relationship with anyone else?

That is very true. Because when you don't take care of yourself; when there is no self-care, the job of caring for you is by implication and expectation handed over to another to do for you. *You* prove to me that I am worth something. That means I have in my head a whole script of tests you have to undertake and pass to validate my being. Only I don't hand you the script. You have to divine it—puzzle it out. So I am licked from the very beginning. You cannot meet expectations that are not explicitly stated. So often a person will say of his partner or mate. "He should have been aware" of something. This is the sheerest nonsense! He could never be aware, no matter how long they had been together. Neither person will ever be aware of the expectations in the other's guts unless those expectations are expressed. The occasional times we guess right are just that—guesses, and cannot be depended upon. They are only lucky hits.

How do you handle tension and
conflicts in the self-care concept?

There are many ways of handling tension. One way is to suffer through it and that may often be necessary. But I would say, first of all, to check out the reality of the tension. If I am pressured—time-pressured on a deadline I have to meet there is tension there that is part of the reality—a reality of things that as a human being I have to face.

There is no such thing as living without tension, without pain. It is simply a part of living. Now part of the *art* of living is, is the tension I am under necessary? And what alternatives do I have to make it easier? It is perfectly true that tensions can sometimes be very productive or creative in the sense of using it as a push into action. When I know that a job of work has to be done within a certain time period, I get it done. It may be a struggle to do it, but this is the created power I must build to do what I don't want to do in order to accomplish something that needs to be done. This is another illustration of expanding ourselves beyond a self-centered immediate desire in order to attain a bigger goal.

*I am completely bogged down in
my relationship with my spouse. I
can't express my anger. If I do, my
partner considers it a personal
attack. Criticizing or being angry at
him prevents him from being
somebody. But not expressing it
prevents me from being somebody.
How can we get out of this
impasse?*

The first job I see for both of you is to come to terms
with the fact that anger is legitimate. And neither
criticism nor anger prevents anybody from being a
somebody. How you handle this acid is the determinant.
You are two human beings and far from angels. As two
human beings you will be enraged at yourself and at each
other because of the limitations that we necessarily have
to face in living, and the misunderstandings that
inevitably happen, unrealized expectations, all of which
contribute to feelings of anger, rage and hostility.

Now, what do we do with it? We can destroy each
other with this rage, or we can use this rage both as a
release and as information-giving. If you say to one
another that your rage is legitimate and that you want to
get information out of it that will decrease the sabotage
of your feelings, then you say to each other, "Look, I
want you to hear me in order to find where I am and just
listen." If there is good feeling between you, we can
make a pact to listen to our rage.

How?

By saying, "Look, I feel angry and hostile. Will you listen to me?" And if you get permission, you are limited by the amount of hostility and anger that the permission-giver can tolerate. So if I give you permission to rage because our relationship is based upon good will and a commitment to be with one another because we want to be with one another, then I could say to you, "I will listen to your anger for one minute, or two minutes and that is as much as I can absorb."

When I give you permission to rage, I know that I'm not going to get a bouquet of roses tossed to me. I know that this is going to be acid; therefore, I have to be sure in my own guts that I can be able to listen, or that I will be willing to listen without contaging your anger. Because when I give you permission to listen, I am frustrating myself from response by mutual agreement. So my response is outlawed by the pact we have made just to listen. A rage release must be separated by time to cool off before we can negotiate our differences. Then we must open our ears to really hear, and listen and deal with the content, the specific issues that have been uncovered.

This kind of liberty, limitation, and discipline
are only possible and workable if there is good
will between the people and a commitment to the
relationship. Both of these mean they are committed to
work at the relationship, and working at the relationship
means dealing with each other's irrationalities and
accumulated steam, in order to make these phenomena
as little damaging as possible and to open productive
roads to a possible increase in harmony.

That makes sense, but one of our problems is that we both have very short fuses. He will lose his temper and say some cruel things and is over it. But the damage has been done and my feelings are hurt or I'm angry. I don't know if either one of us could stop ourselves in order to negotiate this agreement. What do you do about short fuses?

Again, it depends upon your compassion for one another—upon your real significance to one another and your discipline. And remember that what is said itself need not be lethal. It is how what is said is interpreted. You could, by mutual agreement, turn these so-called short fuses into permissible, person-specific ways of letting off steam. So when you say to yourself "When the other blows his fuse, Mt. Vesuvius is errupting," this becomes a process by which you disengage yourself emotionally from the other's acid. We add to this the understanding that such a release will be followed by a rational confrontation on the real issues involved.

What about my hostile feelings?
How can I get away from the
inability to express hostile feelings?

I question that it is an "inability" to express hostile feelings. It may be a conditioned no-no. Simply enough, you can only get away from refraining from expressing hostility by expressing it! This is not an easy job. It entails putting into words the feeling you have. It takes courage to say what you feel and still to say it in a manner that gets heard. Confining yourself to "I" messages is an excellent technique: "I feel abused" "I feel disappointed" "I feel let-down."

But use judgment in expressing hostility. If you say from now on I'm going to validate myself and every time I feel hostile I'm going to express it, you may find yourself in deep trouble. If you express hostility without restraint to your boss, it is almost guaranteed that you will lose your job.

What I'm saying is there are many areas in living when you may not express your hostility. So what do you do? This is why a person-specific decision is absolutely necessary. Instead of getting emotional indigestion on the steam which you can't ventilate to the specific target, you can go to the bathroom and say there what you'd like to say—but safely. You can jog around the block. You can find someplace to go and let out the steam in a very person-specific way.

In Japan, in industrial concerns, there is a room which contains a facsimile of the boss, and the employees go in and pound and punch at. This is a very interesting recognition of the fact that people do get frustrated and that hostility and anger are legitimate, recognized phenomena.

*Throughout the first half of my life
I felt like somebody. I was a
student, I was a wife, then a
mother. I accomplished all those
things and loved doing it. Now my
children are grown and gone and I
feel useless and hopeless and
empty. What can I do?*

First I would say to focus on what doors you can
reopen or what new doors can you open? Focus on a
specific. Dare to take a chance of exploration. Where do
you want to explore? Before you were in the role of wife
and mother you did something else. What else did you
do?

I was a secretary. But my skills are so rusty that I would feel embarrassed to be in an employment office with a lot of people half my age. I don't think anyone would hire a grey-haired lady.

You may be barred in some organizations because of age, and welcomed in others for the same reason. Research has shown that the mature woman is more stable, more dependable on the job, so there are doors you could open. You say your skills are rusty. How important is this to you? Important enough to invest at practicing whatever skills you feel rusty in, daily, on a time-budget basis in order to re-acquire them: Re-learning takes less time than learning, and you may be amazed at the speed at which you can pick up on a skill.

*I guess my basic probem is that I
don't feel needed anymore.*

When you think of need in terms of another's
dependence on you—that the other cannot get along
without you, this is only true when your children are
really helpless and unable to do for themselves. Being
necessary to another person is obviously for a limited
length of time. If your importance is dependent upon
another's need of you, what you are saying is, "I am of no
value unless I can serve in a familiar role." This is very,
very limited interest and limited concept of the human
being, and very self-limiting. What you are saying is that
you no longer feel important, because to feel important
means to have impact, and to have impact means to
develop an interest in something that has meaning. So
what you are really into is finding a new meaning in your
life other than the limitations of specific roles. Many of
us forget that parenting is by its very nature a time-
limited job. So preparations for an empty nest should
start, realistically, when the nest is first filled. But it is
never too late to utilize your resources. Look into the
world around you and become part of it in whatever
interests you can find—social, educational, religious,
economic, or political. As long as you are alive and
breathing there is the possibility of growth. Whether or
not you want to put that into action is your decision.
Again, we're into an investment of time, energy, and
work. Are you worth this investment?

*I am a very shy person. I'm through
school now, and I have to get a job.
But the very thought of going out
on interviews terrifies me. Yet
I have to do it. What can I do?*

You have many options, one of which is practicing doing the very thing you fear doing. We can do this either in psychodrama or we could go on a fantasy trip.

For example, visualize yourself going into a particular building, going to a particular door. Visualize yourself going through that door, presenting yourself to the secretary for the appointment that has already been made. Visualize the possible employer and start presenting yourself for the job. Assess your assets—what you have to sell, show him why he should be interested in hiring you. Research all your resources and verbalize them. Write a script for yourself and go through the scenes as if you were participating in a TV show. Go through this fantasy trip again and again and again. Go through all the motions. Find yourself driving to the place of the appointment. Go through it all. And make your sales pitch.

How would I use psychodrama?

You would use your friends. Write the entire script in your mind, and assign them parts. One could be the very austere, no-nonsense employer who is interested not in you as a personality, but what you can produce and how you can produce.

Set up your projected interview by use of friends as a surrogate boss, surrogate secretary, surrogate receptionist and you present yourself to each in turn. Play each scene a little differently. Give different characterizations to the players, so you develop practice in a variety of personality-meetings.

What you are doing here is what I had the architect do in my practice. You are deliberately exposing yourself to something you either dislike or fear. Making yourself familiar with the very thing that turns you off, decreases the fear, the hate, the extreme reaction to whatever it is. In this case, it is your fear of employment interviews. To become familiar with what you fear may be the antidote to the sabotage of an avoidance you want to overcome.

*As a kid I always wanted to
accomplish something just beyond
me. I didn't learn fast enough and
it wasn't worth the time and effort.
Now I seem to have trouble setting
any kind of goal for myself. What
do I do about goals and achieving
them?*

Everything depends upon the realism of the goal you
set for yourself. For instance, a realistic goal for a
youngster might be to finish elementary school. But for
the mentally retarded or someone suffering from brain
damage, that would be a very unrealistic goal. If I want
to be a great dancer, but have no physical coordination,
that would be an unrealistic goal, obviously.

What would you like to have happen or accomplish?
What is the daily task needed to meet that goal? Then
test out the personal fit. I would hope to accomplish two
things: to test the personal fit and to keep myself from
losing the joy of living in the day, instead of
concentrating only in the future or only in the past. Never
lose the joy of *living in the day.* And if you find the day
miserable in itself, then you'd better do some fast self-
examination.

Another aspect of this is the man whose goal is to accumulate economic wealth, with the expectation that this will bring happiness. And in the process of accumulation, he neglects his wife, family, and all other interests. This makes the attainment of the goal very barren and disappointing because he hasn't built the resources to enjoy the fruits of his labor.

If you are serious about developing your talents, assess the investment this would entail. The work of creation is based on much discipline. Patience and persistence are requisites. Somehow, I suspect you might be seeking the diploma before investing in the course of study.

*I am in hiding. I have spent a
lifetime in hiding. Nothing I ever
do with or in front of other people
works out. If I try to tell a joke or a
story, it seems flat and stupid.
If I have to speak at any length to
someone more accomplished than I
am, my thoughts and ideas seem
worthless. More and more I seem to
be covered by a thick shell that
blocks me from the world. What
can I do to feel the touch of
humanity?*

Get rid of the disapproving judge who sits on your
shoulder. You placed him there. You can throw him off.

Stop being so competitive. Stop measuring yourself
against somebody brighter, wiser, more erudite, or
whatever. Give yourself the right to be yourself.

You measure yourself against outside criteria.
Someone is brighter than you, so you are stupid and
worth nothing. That's an interesting conclusion. Does
someone else's talent depreciate you? In truth, there are
many ways in which you are brighter than I; there are
many ways in which I am more than you in other aspects.
Since we start with the basic premise that as human
beings, we are not perfect, so we come to terms with the
fact that we have adequacies and inadequacies. If I can
relate to you only by comparing my strengths and
weaknesses against yours—how can we have a

relationship? But if I can relate to you by simply sharing our common humanness, we can have a glorious relationship. I can enjoy your strengths, and you can enjoy my strengths, and maybe we can both laugh at each other's weaknesses. There can be something endearing in forgetting a punch line. I can say that I'm a lousy story-teller, but this struck me as funny, and then I tell the story and get nothing but blank looks at the end of it. We can still both enjoy the experience. This is part of what I mean by taking the right to be. It is conceivable that the other person doesn't expect you to be a Class A comedian, but enjoys the fact that you can or can't tell a joke. We have each special idiosyncracies, and when we deal with each other we acknowledge them, and live around them, we free each other to relate as human beings. So, because I can't tell a story dramatically does not mean I should shut my mouth. Because you may be more erudite than I doesn't mean I don't have valuable opinions to verbalize. And as I verbalize and engage in an interchange, I am already engaged in the process of growth because I have opened myself up to new ideas and to clarifying my own thoughts through the very process of talking. Not talking is a deliberate sabotage of one's self. It makes one's self immobile. There has to be movement to grow and that involves again the risk of error. Error—when used productively—ensures further growth.

I have been married for 20 years
and I am unhappy and I know that
the marriage is over. I know I have
to make a decision. How do I get
the courage to make a decision and
how do I know it is the right one?

In the first place, if you wait for the courage to make a decision, you will immobilize yourself. And if you can live only on certainty, you are going to remain stationary. There is no certainty. Every decision is a risk. There is no way of knowing outside of testing the doing dependent upon the decision you make. There is no guarantee that any decision you make is the "right" decision.

If you wait for the courage to break a relationship, perhaps you are waiting for something that is unattainable. And when you decide to break a relationship, if that is the decision, you carry it out no matter how much you quake inside, and you carry out such a decision based upon as realistic an assessment as you can make. You say to yourself, "The price of the relationship is too high for me to pay. Therefore, as an act of self-care, I have to break the relationship in order to grow as a human being and free myself to be me— whatever the "me" is."

And if you make a decision and are unhappy with it, you can always make another decision. You have to assess the fruitfulness of whatever relationship you are in. What does it do for me and what does it do against me? And if it wipes me out as a person, then I make the decision to make a change, and any change is painful. This could be true of a relationship between a man and a woman, it could be your mother living with you, it could be a grown son who has stuck around too long. An unknown is what is involved—and an unknown by its very nature is fearful. At least the misery you have is familiar, and what is familiar is not usually fearful to us. There is less fear in the known, even if it is an unhappy known.

*You say that self-care will lead "to
acceptance of one's self as a human
being. As a human being you will
love and hate, be constructive and
sometimes destructive, be serene
and at times tempestuous, rational
and irrational—but always* you *in
the many facets of you." Is it okay
to do negative things?*

I would put it differently. It is *human* to do negative
things. Now, how can we productively deal with what it is
human to do? Now, if my impetuousness has gotten me
into deep trouble, then how do I get out of it?
Realistically. Say, "Okay, I made a mess. Now, what can
I do about it and what can I learn from it? This turns the
mess into a growth process, handled this way. Not that
the *mess* is positive; of course it is not. Every mess is
negative. But as a human being, you will make your
messes. So what do you do? Sit and brood about it, or do
you use it as a learning process? "I will not be this
impulsive again. It took too much work and energy to get
myself out of this. So I'll think twice about going off half-
cocked again."

That is what I mean when I say, no experience is wasted, provided you make it a learning experience. And a learning experience means not duplicating the original mess. But you will make messes. That is one of the rare things I can guarantee. Dealing with them productively can make each mess occur less frequently and be less destructive.

*I just lost my husband. I am
absolutely bereft and shocked and
unable to face anything. My whole
life was wrapped up in this man
and now it's all over. How am I
going to get through this?*

There is no way of erasing the pain that you feel; the
frustration, the grief. The only thing I know is that time
will decrease the suffering. In spite of all the pain and
grief and agony—you start with the decision that you are
going to live. That is already a productive decision. Now,
in spite of the grief and the agony, what are the ways
in which you can, first, immediately live with some
degree of comfort? So you have the very realistic job of
self-care. The grieving time can be a reaping time—
reaping the treasures of friendships and family
associations. Make use of them. Don't be reluctant to
call on them for company, for emotional nourishment
and for change of focus on your part, and that's your
responsibility. Since you've decided to live, how can you
get through each day in spite of the pain, accomplishing
something for yourself. Even if it is the agony of cleaning
out drawers and closets of what is no longer useful. And
what you are saying is, I am relinquishing what is past to
open room for something new I can create. The truth is
that, of course, transition is painful, but the pain is not
everlasting and continuously ongoing, providing you
don't nourish it. In the decision to live there are certain
minimal things you have to do in order to live. Research

yourself and environment. Commit yourself to a series of smaller and larger decision-making processes. What I am really saying is, accept the fact that no individual is indispensable to another's living. We can live with all kinds of deprivations and create new emotional wealth for ourselves. The process is painful, and an inevitable part of living.

You utilize friends, because friends are there to use, not to abuse, but to use—to help you over a period of time that is very difficult. If you have family at home, then focus on their interests as a means of freeing yourself, changing focus from the agony you feel into the need of another person. A change of focus is vital, whether it is the change of focus into the interest or well-being of another person, doing for another person, or changing focus in preparation of work that needs to be done anyway.

Or, as we said earlier, open new avenues to explore. Don't stop yourself from grieving, but don't get enmeshed in *just* grieving. Make room for *doing* in the grieving.

*In your dealing with people—all
the thousands of people you have
helped individually and collectively,
do you ever get a sense of awe about
the fact that you have this power,
this intuitive seeing power into
people?*

Not at all. Because what I make clear and what I firmly believe is that you are responsible for your life and *I don't have this power over you.* Whatever change is made, *you* are making it. And I always make quite clear that you take anything I say and fit it on for size—for person-specific fit. If it doesn't fit you as a person—if it doesn't lay well in your guts—you discard it.

So, when I say to you, here are possible alternatives, you choose one which fits you. I simply indicate that there are doors to open.

What doors you open are your responsibility, not mine.

I never confuse myself with God.

HOW TO BE SOMEBODY

It is your job to:

* Risk being authentic—self-respecting *as if* you were worth an investment of work,
* To take the right to say I am not available to you at this time,
* To take the courage to include yourself when you feel "left out,"
* To accept your right to goof, and dedicate yourself to utilizing your goofs as learning processes,
* To risk decision-making,
* To accommodate at times as an act of self-expansion,
* To allow expressions of pride in yourself,
* To be open about what has nurturing meaning to you.

It is your job also, to:

* Assess the many ways and means you tie yourself
  in knots, research ways and means of freeing
  yourself from self-imposed constrictions, self-
  limitations, sabotages (oughts, shoulds,
  must-nots),
* Judge only to change, not to deprecate,
* Risk engaging in self-validating behavior.
* Assign yourself the specifics of the above.
* Give yourself the *right* to be.
* *Dare* to be.
* Take responsibility for self-care.
And finally, to be somebody means:
* I have attained impact on my world.
* I feel important!
* I count!
* I have self-worth, self-liking, and self-respect.